W9-AAT-941

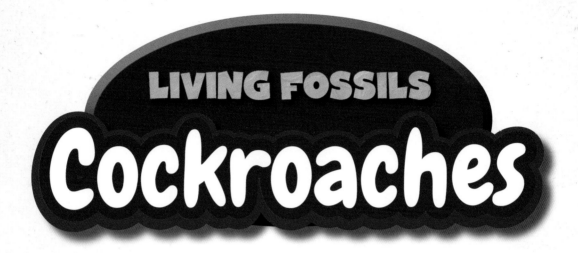

LIVING FOSSILS
Cockroaches

Sarah Machajewski

PowerKiDS
press.

New York

Published in 2015 by The Rosen Publishing Group, Inc.
29 East 21st Street, New York, NY 10010

First Edition

Editor: Sarah Machajewski
Book Design: Mickey Harmon

Photo Credits: Cover, pp. 1–24 (border) Markus Gann/Shutterstock.com; cover (logo texture), pp. 1–4, 6, 8–10, 12, 14, 16, 20, 22–24 (background texture) Bplanet/Shutterstock.com; cover (foreground cockroaches) skydie/Shutterstock.com; cover (background cockroaches) Smit/Shutterstock.com; p. 4 Robert Eastman/Shutterstock.com; p. 5 Scientifica/Visuals Unlimited, Inc./Visuals Unlimited/Getty Images; p. 7 (top) aopsan/Shutterstock.com; p. 7 (bottom) Dr. Morley Read/Shutterstock.com; p. 9 Kosin Sukhum/Shutterstock.com; p. 11 smuay/Shutterstock.com; p. 13 Barnaby Chambers/Shutterstock.com; p. 15 (top) D. Kucharski K. Kucharska/Shutterstock.com; p. 15 (bottom) Bates Littlehales/Contributor/National Geographic/Getty Images; p. 17 ShaunWilkinson/Thinkstock.com; pp. 18, 19 Jan Stromme/Stone/Getty Images; p. 21 (bottom) Michael McCoy/Photo Researchers/Getty Images; p. 21 (top) Aleksey Stemmer/Shutterstock.com; p. 22 CHOKCHAI POOMICHAIYA/Shutterstock.com.

Library of Congress Cataloging-in-Publication Data

Machajewski, Sarah, author.
 Cockroaches / Sarah Machajewski.
     pages cm. — (Living fossils)
 Includes bibliographical references and index.
ISBN 978-1-4777-5811-3 (pbk.)
ISBN 978-1-4777-5814-4 (6 pack)
ISBN 978-1-4777-5813-7 (library binding)
1. Cockroaches—Juvenile literature. 2. Living fossils—Juvenile literature. I. Title.
 QL505.5.M33 2015
 595.7'28—dc23
                                        2014030413

Manufactured in the United States of America

CPSIA Compliance Information: Batch #CW15PK: For Further Information contact Rosen Publishing, New York, New York at 1-800-237-9932

Contents

The Ancient Cockroach

Cockroaches—they're creepy! They're crawly. They're also very, very old. These ancient **arthropods** have been on Earth for over 300 million years. They've changed so little in that time that it would be hard to tell a modern cockroach from one that lived hundreds of millions of years ago.

The cockroach has survived without needing to change the way it looks, what it eats, or how it lives. All these **traits** were suited to both the ancient world and today. Most people think they're gross or even scary, but cockroaches are our planet's greatest survivors!

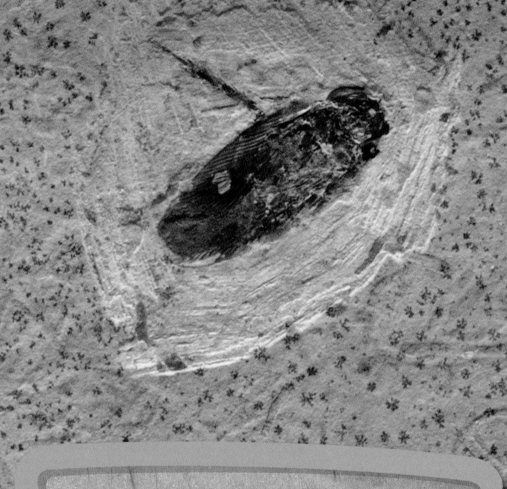

Cockroaches today look much like the fossil, or hardened remains, of this cockroach, which lived millions of years ago.

Small Insect, Big Numbers

Cockroaches belong to a group of insects called Blattodea (blah-TOH-dee-yuh). Their **ancestors** were in a group called Blattoptera, which also includes ancestors of mantids and termites. This ancient family tree goes farther back than the dinosaurs!

There are about 4,500 species, or kinds, of cockroaches around the world. They live everywhere you can imagine, except in polar regions and the tops of mountains. Cockroaches are best known for how they **invade** where people live, but only about 30 species ever come into contact with humans. Of these, only four are considered pests.

FOSSIL FACTS

The four cockroach species that are considered pests are the American cockroach, German cockroach, Oriental cockroach, and brown-banded cockroach.

Cockroaches live in forests, jungles, deserts, swamps, plains, valleys, meadows, fields, and more. They also live in our homes, restaurants, and city buildings. Yuck!

Examining the Cockroach

Although many kinds of bugs look much like the cockroach, there's no mistaking one when you see it. Its oval-shaped body, antennae, and six legs have been part of the cockroach's body for ages.

A cockroach's body has three sections: the head, the **thorax**, and the **abdomen**. You can't see much of a cockroach's head when you look at it from above. Its head points downward, but that doesn't mean it's always looking down. A cockroach has **compound eyes**. Each eye has over 1,000 lenses. This allows a cockroach to see in all directions, which helps it sense when danger is coming.

FOSSIL FACTS

Antennae are long body parts used as feelers and as a way for a cockroach to smell. They can be as long as a cockroach's body.

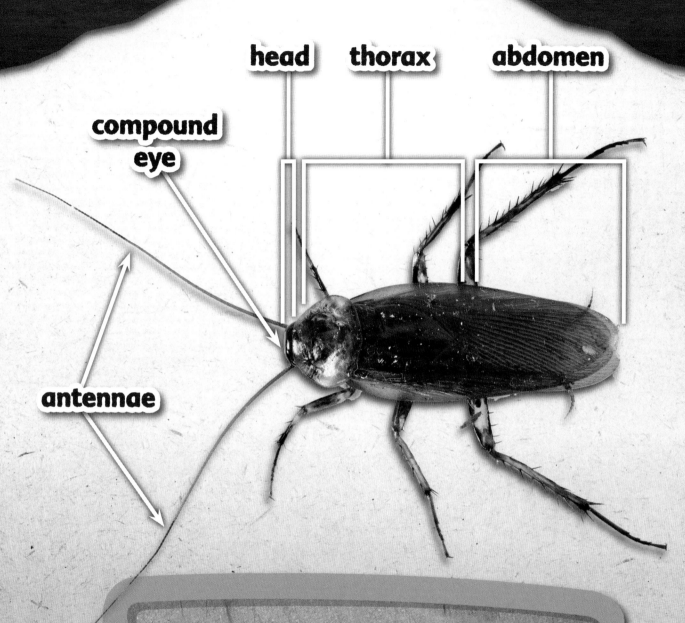

head   **thorax**   **abdomen**

**compound
eye**

antennae

Cockroaches have an exoskeleton, which is a hard
outer covering that protects an insect's body.
Some cockroaches have wings, but not all can fly.

9

Run Away!

Cockroaches are known for scurrying, something their special legs make possible. Three pairs of legs are connected to the thorax. The legs closest to the head are the shortest. They act like brakes. The second pair is used to speed up or slow down. The third pair moves the cockroach forward.

The abdomen houses most of a cockroach's **organs**, as well as something very important—the cerci. Cerci are small hairs on the abdomen's underside that help a cockroach sense things around it. The cerci are so **sensitive** that they can pick up on the tiniest movement of air.

FOSSIL FACTS

A cockroach can run about 50 body lengths in one second. That's the same as a human running 200 miles (320 km) per hour!

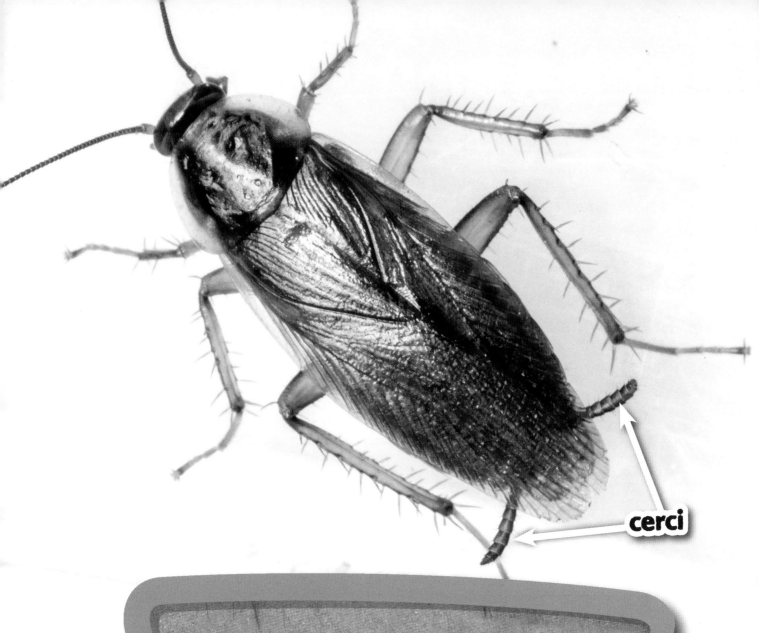

cerci

The cerci and legs are the cockroach's most important defenses. The cerci sense any movement around the cockroach, and the legs help it run away—quickly!

A Scavenger's Supper

What would life be like if you could eat everything around you? That's the life of a cockroach. Cockroaches are scavengers, which means they eat anything they can find, including dead animals and plants.

Cockroaches eat everything—food, wood, paper, glue, soap, and more. You name it, and cockroaches eat it. Imagine how helpful this has been to their survival. In all the time they've been on Earth, cockroaches have never had to worry about a lack of food. It's one thing that's helped them survive, but it also means they'll go anywhere for food, including our homes.

FOSSIL FACTS

Cockroaches bite, chew, and grind their food thanks to mouthparts that act like teeth. However, cockroaches don't use their mouth to breathe. They breathe through tiny holes, called spiracles, on the sides of their body.

Cockroaches **digest** food in their abdomen. Their body can break down anything they take in.

13

The Species Grows

Does the world need any more cockroaches? Cockroaches think so, which is why they mate, or come together to make babies. Female cockroaches make a special odor to draw male cockroaches. Then, the females lay egg cases called oothecae (oh-uh-THEE-kee). Oothecae carry between 15 to 50 eggs each. The eggs **develop** into tiny cockroaches, which work together to break out of the egg case.

Baby cockroaches are called nymphs. They're born white and soft, but gain color and become hard after a few hours. Nymphs grow into adult cockroaches by molting. Molting is when they shed their outer skin. Cockroaches stop molting when they become adults.

FOSSIL FACTS

Female cockroaches lay their oothecae in dark places that are safe from danger. They use their saliva, or spit, to stick the egg case to a hard surface.

molting cockroach

An adult cockroach lives for about one year.

ootheca

nymphs

Community Living

Cockroaches are sneaky creatures that hide in dark corners and scurry away once they're spotted. However, if you've seen one, it's almost certain there are hundreds or even thousands more where it came from.

Cockroaches are very social insects. They live together in large groups. Each cockroach community has a special smell cockroaches can use to recognize each other. Cockroaches also leave a scent trail in their waste, which tells other cockroaches where to find food and water. Scientists believe cockroach nymphs need to grow up around other cockroaches in order to develop correctly.

Cockroaches work together to find food, water, and suitable places to live. Working together allows these insects to grow and survive.

Infested!

Cockroach communities are good for cockroaches, but bad for us. Large groups of cockroaches that invade human spaces are called infestations. Infestations are bad because some cockroaches carry germs that can make us sick.

Our best defense against cockroaches is to keep our living spaces clean and keep food and water out of their reach.

Cockroaches will do whatever they can to get to their food. They can squeeze their bodies into cracks that are only 1/16 of an inch (1.6 mm) wide! Once cockroaches are in, it may seem like they're there to stay. They can survive nearly anything, including having their head pulled off! Are you surprised this species has survived for hundreds of millions of years?

FOSSIL FACTS

Cockroaches can escape anything—except their predators. They include wasps, centipedes, toads, birds, and more.

In the Wild

Cockroaches get a bad name from the few species that live among us. But there are thousands of cockroaches we'll never see, and some of them are really cool. The Madagascar hissing cockroach lives on the island of Madagascar, which is part of Africa. Males have horns, which they use to battle other males. During the fight, they let out a loud hiss. Winning cockroaches usually hiss more than losing cockroaches.

The giant burrowing cockroach is the heaviest cockroach in the world. It weighs about 1 ounce (30 g). It digs into the soils of Australia, where it makes its home. These cockroaches don't bother humans at all.

FOSSIL FACTS

Cockroaches can actually help us. Their waste carries a gas called nitrogen. Soil takes in nitrogen, which helps grow healthy plants. That helps us all!

Madagascar hissing cockroach

These cockroaches would rather hide in nature than bother us!

giant burrowing cockroach

No End in Sight

The cockroach is one of the most **resourceful** creatures in the world. It feeds on almost everything. It can make a home in nature, but also lives in walls, pipes, and cardboard boxes. Its eyes see in all directions, its cerci pick up on any hint of danger, and its legs help it escape quickly. It doesn't even die right away when it loses its head!

These traits and more have kept cockroaches around for hundreds of millions of years. There's no end in sight for this fascinating species. It outlived the dinosaurs, and it may just outlive humans, too!

Glossary

abdomen: The part of an animal's body that contains the stomach.

ancestor: An animal that lived before others in its family tree.

arthropod: Any of a group of animals with jointed legs, a hard outer covering, and no backbone.

compound eye: An animal's eye made up of several repeating units that are used to see.

defense: Something used to protect oneself.

develop: To grow or mature.

digest: To break down food.

invade: To enter in large numbers.

organ: A collection of tissues that has a specific function, such as a stomach.

resourceful: Having the ability to overcome challenges.

sensitive: Quick to pick up on and respond to slight changes.

thorax: The section of an insect's body that contains the heart and lungs.

trait: A feature that is passed on for generations of animals.

Index

A
abdomen, 8, 9, 10, 13
antennae, 8, 9
arthropods, 4

C
cerci, 10, 11, 22
compound eyes, 8, 9, 22

D
defenses, 11, 18

E
eggs, 14
exoskeleton, 9

H
head, 8, 9, 10, 19, 22

I
infestations, 18

L
legs, 8, 10, 11, 22

M
mate, 14
molting, 14, 15
mouth, 12

N
nymphs, 14, 15, 16

O
oothecae, 14, 15

P
pests, 6
predators, 19

S
scavengers, 12
social insects, 16
species, 6, 19, 20, 22
spiracles, 12

T
thorax, 8, 9, 10

Websites

Due to the changing nature of Internet links, PowerKids Press has developed an online list of websites related to the subject of this book. This site is updated regularly. Please use this link to access the list: www.powerkidslinks.com/fos/ckrc